Nine Lives

Nine Lives

By Kayla Delcoure

The Pawtistics, LLC
2025

Kayla Delcoure

thepawtistics.com

Nine Lives

Copyright © 2025 Kayla Delcoure

ISBN hardback: 979-8-9986880-2-7

ISBN paperback: 979-8-9986880-1-0

ISBN ebook: 979-8-9986880-0-3

First Edition

Dedication

*To Gizmo and every person
who loved him with me*

Table of Contents

The Void

Hi, there, dear Reader.
Have you seen my fluffy void?
Here. She looks like this:

Twinkles

Once upon a time,
when my son was four years old,
he didn't know what whiskers were
and had never been told.

He saw them on his soul cat, Bruce,
and tried his best to say
how much he loved his cat's
                    "twinkles"
so that's their name today!

Marbles

Empty noggin.
No one home.
Only marbles
in that dome.

Little Furmaid

Look at this fluff.
Isn't he neat?

Wouldn't you say that
my fluff's got cute feet?

Wouldn't you think
he's a squirrel?

A squirrel who has,
everything.

Fan Mail

Hello, down there.
I hope you're well.
Is it your turn to use the cell?

Oh–

Please don't look at me like that.
You're not meant to touch me, cat.

My blades are dull, but they move quick.
Not even your big head's that thick.

I'm still not quite sure why you yell.
Will spinning break your screaming spell?

I wish you luck with your big plans.

Love from above,
Your Ceiling Fan

Home At Last

"A new girl showed up.
Maybe this one will keep me.
Outside is no home."

– Arya (2012)

Purrkour!

Floor

Wall

Floor

It's called kitty purrkour.

Every. Time.

What's that in your fur?
Come here. Let me check real quick.
No, don't you dare run!

Cat Parades

Up the hall and down the hall,
a loud

THUD

as one hits a wall.

Not horses, hippos, hand grenades.
Just nightly upstairs cat parades.

Bring Them With

Eight moves in five years.
Crossing coast to coast four times.
Now, we rest our paws.

Crinkle Rainbow

Crinkle toy in the sky.
It can fly twice as high.
Take a look,
'cause he is shook.
It's taunting Floki.

Airplane Mode

Head full of beans.
Braincell won't load.
Time to turn on
airplane mode.

Tray table up.
Seat back upright.
Zoomies that last
the entire night.

Kisses

Behind the ears
for all the times
you've listened to me
when no one else would.

On the forehead
for all the times
you believed in me
when I doubted I could.

Over the heart
for all the times
you loved me
when I thought no one should.

The Brain and the Fluff

"Okay, Fluff,
now listen here—
I'm going to say this
nice and clear.

Go be weird
close to the boys;
rear your head and
smack their toys.

They'll get distracted
from their food
to watch you in
your silly mood.

Make them laugh
so they can't see,
as I swipe their nugs
for you and me."

It's the Law

I sleep on Mom
without a care.
She cannot move,
for she is chair.

Colors

Roses are red,
violets are [also] red.
Colors aren't real
in a feline head.

Bathroom Penguin

Welcome in to
bathroom time.
My name's Bruce.
This bathroom's mine.

I'll sit politely
in my suit
while you sit there
and call me cute.

Forehead Kisses

Five kisses on the head,
the nightly lullaby.
In return, slow blinks and purrs,
until the morning's nigh.

Take Your Meds

You take yours. I take mine.
That's what we do at bed-med time.

Kayla Delcoure

Trigger Warning:

The following poems contain intense, raw emotions and
explore themes of loss, grief, and healing.
Reader discretion is advised.

To bypass triggering content, skip to page 65.
(It's okay to not be ready yet.)

Drama

"All this drama over a cat."

You don't understand.
He carried my soul.

Anticipatory grief:

when you see the Reaper check its watch.

Hollow

I watched the Reaper for one month.
The clock it brought was deafening.
The second hand moved slower
than the hour most days.

Every night at the foot of my bed,
it sat there waiting. The incessant
tapping of its foot kept me awake.

Death was impatient.

Tick, tock, tick, tock.

The Reaper was stubborn,

but so was Gizmo

        until the clock stopped.

Death left me hollow.

Unfair

I can't take it.
I need you here.
My world's not bright
without you near.

Statistically, this shouldn't be.
You should be safe from FIP.

The golden light
of breaking dawn
is not as bright.

My Sunshine's gone.

Untimely

Food demanded at the
precise hour.

Bedtime the same every
night. YELLING if I'm late.

A life built around a
clock

and yet,

his death was

untimely.

Tick, tock, tick.

Writing on the Walls

I sat with my memories,
learned the names of my
nightmares. I had to get
the thoughts out.

I stayed in the dark so long
my eyes adjusted—
enough to read the words
carved into the walls of my skull.

Not fair.
Not fair.
Not fair.

HE SHOULD STILL BE HERE.

The Truth?

The truth?

I miss who I was before part of me died with him.

Empty

I didn't eat for three days.
I'm not sure if
I breathed,
but I know I didn't eat.

It didn't bring him back.

The spiral of a sad girl:

If I change the name,
it will be like he was never here.

If I change the name,
they won't know he was real.

I can't slosh off this
festering anger.
Tears in my eyes.
Fire in my lungs.
Salt in my wounds.

He should still be here.

Humans were never meant
to mourn in front of millions.
And I was never meant
to lose him so young.

Sometimes I wish my channels
were about turtles so it would
make more sense to hide in my shell.

Reflection

My office has been a mess
since you left.

Ten months now.

A mirror of my mind.

If I clean it, I will see exactly how much

s p a c e

you took up in my happiest place,
and how much silence now
           hangs.

Even Now

I cry with my whole self
when I cry for him.
My body quakes.
Jaws lock.

The lines on my face that once formed
from his humor now deepen from

each

sharp

heave

through grinding teeth.

My heart climbs so high in
my throat that I choke on my sobs.
Buckled over. Eyes shut.

I don't want to see a world without his light.

They All Say

"Everything happens for a reason."

No.

The universe is impulsive
and morally desolate.
Fairness doesn't matter
in a world built for beasts.

"What doesn't kill you makes you stronger."

No.

What doesn't kill you can still
whip you so raw that
you welcome the itch of scabs,
because at least you know

you're healing.

The Library

Inside the library of my old videos,

the shelves are lined
with joyous memories,
but every page turn is another
papercut reminder of my future
without him.

Nights like tonight I feel my soul
tearing at its bindings all over again.
The stitching never healed.
The glue never dried.

Nights like tonight feel like all
my pages will f a l l
                    o
                     u
                      t
                       .

Pity

Pity those who cast ridicule
as you mourn your beloved.

They have never felt the love
that makes the pain worth it.

It Hurts

I miss him infinitely.
Pictures hurt.
Videos feel like
sledgehammers.
His songs that once
lifted my spirits
now sink my heart.

The rage I once felt is gone.
Therapized out of me–
a demon of my design.
But the ache of that
missing piece of my soul
burns.

I miss him fiercely and
nothing can bring him back.
No amount of happy memories
can soothe the fact that
                    Floki is now older than him.

Time shouldn't work like that.

Bargaining

What I would give
to hear his voice again.

Ashes

A piece of my heart is
in his ashes.
Nothing has filled the pit
where Gizmo's love once lived.

Scar tissue grows

slowly.

I am *desperate*
to feel whole again.

The cavity he made
echoes with his memories
at every beat.

The "Before" Smile

A picture is worth one thousand words.

But one thousand pictures aren't enough
to make me smile like I did before
I lost you.

Changes

I moved my couch.
I changed the rug.
I cannot step
where we last hugged.

I sent my sweater
off with you.
I know it was
your favorite too.

The sun shines
where we said
goodbye.
Each day, I still
can see you die.

Glimpses of You

I saw you
in his fur tonight.
He looks like you
in warm, dim light.

With things about
and chores to do,
Tonight I chose to
sit with you.

Still

I think about you
every day.
Hoping it will hurt less.

(It doesn't.)

Happiness*

After you lose a pet,
they promise you
you'll be happy again.

What they don't tell you,
is that *your happiness
will never be the same.

Expectation vs. Reality

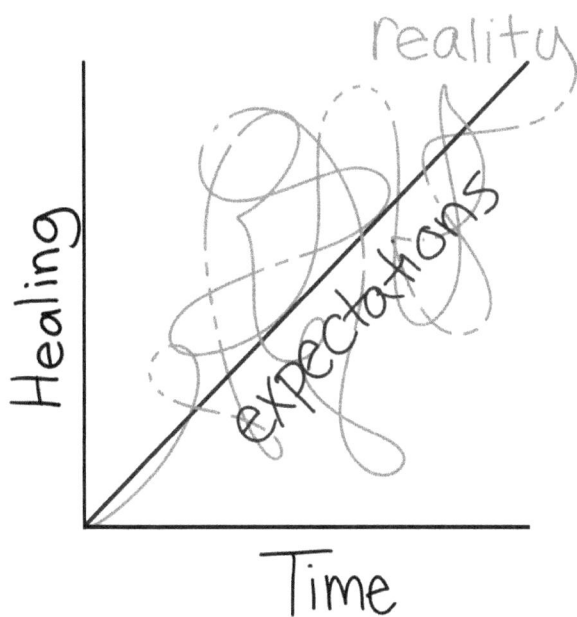

Remember Him

I changed my profile pic today
to Floki 'cause he fits.
But with that move,
I cannot soothe
the fear that they'll
forget.

Golden Hour

All six of them here in one room.

Quiet

warmth

peace in tune.

The setting sun breathes golden light.
This is the place my heart feels right.

Sleep Spots

Every night when I'm in bed,
Arya rests right by my head.

The penguin sleeps down at my feet,
between the top and fitted sheet.

The window hammock holds the void,
usually with her favorite toy.

The tiger twins sleep on the wall,
one in a bin so he won't fall.

The fluffy moose sleeps on a bed,
not in it, but on top instead.

At night, all six sleep in our room.
And when they wake, it's time to zoom.

And Then I Lost Her

I was lost in a book
when Floki crept
up to me in bed.

He looked

down at my empty lap,

behind me at the empty pillow,

then at me with one question in his eyes.

"Where is Arya?"

Continuous

Every day I become more convinced
there is no such thing as the past
tense of "heal," only present progressive.

Always healing.

Never healed.

Five Cat Things to See:

1. The tips of his teeth poking out from under his lips

2. The hair on the tips of his ears

3. The color of his nose

Licorice?
  Terra-cotta?
    Bubblegum?

4. The whiskers on the backs of his legs

5. The color of his toe beans

Four Cat Things to Feel:

1. The pressure in your hand when he nudges his head into your palm for attention

2. The texture of his fur

Is it silk? Fluff?

Has it grown coarser from years of snuggling?

3. The weight of his paws on your lap

How can an eight-pound cat suddenly weigh 80 pounds when standing on you with one paw?

4. The velvet softness of his ears

Three Cat Things to Hear:

1. The *pat* *pat* *pat* of his paws
on the ground as he approaches you

2. The way his purring gets louder
when he takes a deep, unguarded breath

3. The *brdrdrdr* activation sound he
makes when you pet him while he's resting

Two Cat Things to Smell:

1. His forehead

2. The side of his face by the base of his ears

One Cat Thing to Taste:

1. Please do not lick your cat

Be Loud

Heal loudly because the
silence is where you suffered.

Bruce Be Nimble

Did
you know
I can climb
a flight of stairs
by only using two steps?

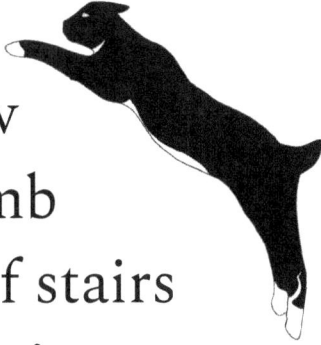

The Tiger Twins

Belly to belly.
Heart to heart.
Awake or asleep,
but never apart.

Strangers by blood.
Brothers by bond.
Brought together
by an Orange beyond.

Oh, Gizmo.
You would have
loved them so much.

Bowling Ball

My tail is thick.
My head is small.
My body is
a bowling ball.

Kayla Delcoure

Loophole

The rule of the house is
no running on stairs.
What Mom didn't ban
was traversing in pairs.

While biting and chasing
and chewing on tails
In the arena of elevation
only one cat prevails.

Surprise

Round head.
Empty eyes.
Every thought
is a surprise.

Snack Time

One eats chicken.
One eats foam.
One eats bread
when no one's home.

One eats grass
and chews on plants.
One likes cardboard.
One eats hands.

Cats in snack order: Arya, Bruce, Floki, Luna, Popper, Mushu

A Leafy Haiku

Where did this leaf go?

...

Luna, did you eat the plant?

I SWEAR TO FLUFF, CAT!!

Popper's Plan

Open mouth.
Inhale air.
Find a shut door.
Scream and stare.

Once inside,
they'll close the door.
Wait 'til they sit,
then scream some more.

Homework Assignment

If you have a cat near you,
look at them now.
Tell them you love them.

Now do that every day forever.

The Nine Lives

Arya
Bruce
Floki
Gizmo
Luna
Me
Mushu
Popper
You

One Last Thing

They never clipped my wings
before they put me in this cell.
All I want to do is fly,
yet I rot in corporate hell.

Now the only height I gain
is on the ladder of this game
and while the world may know my name,
I work my nine to five in chains.

But–

my day will come. It has to.
That's the promise that I keep.
Between my cats, between my heart,
the dreams I want aren't in my sleep.

The sky is thick,
polluted
with dark, concentrated hate.
The only way to brighter days
is to let the birds create.

Acknowledgements

To my husband, Ryan, and our two wonderful children—thank you for walking beside me through whatever-the-heck it is that I'm doing with these cats.

Ryan, your strength continues to hold me up when I fall apart. This collection would not exist without your patience, your hugs, and your ability to see my soul more clearly than anyone else. I am endlessly grateful for everything you do.

To Mom and Dad—thank you for believing in me as I chase my limitless dreams.

To my aunties, Mary and Janice—thank you for your mentorship and love, and for snapping me out of my impostor syndrome when needed. (And an extra thanks, Mary, for editing the collection! *Commas remain my weakness.*)

I am profoundly grateful to the friends and loved ones who held space for my sorrow and never rushed my healing after losing Gizmo. Your compassion gave me the strength to put all these words on pages.

This book is for everyone who has had to say goodbye and is still learning how to live with the echo of that love. I see you.

Kayla Delcoure

Looking for more content?

Cat Comedy & Updates
Bluesky
Facebook
Instagram
Threads
TikTok
YouTube

Behind-the-Scenes Exclusives
Patreon

Pet Loss & Grief Support
www.thepawtistics.com

Online Community
Discord

Press Inquiries
info@thepawtistics.com

PS: Tell your cat I said pspspspsps.
- K